Doggie Devos
Taking "Paws" to Reflect on God's Goodness

DANIKA DEVA & FRIENDS

Doggie Devos Taking "Paws" to Reflect on God's Goodness
Copyright © 2023 Danika Deva
All rights reserved.
ISBN: 9798870334714

BIBLE PERMISSIONS

Cover Design: Heather Hart;
Photography: Sonya Weaver; Sonya Weaver Photography

DEDICATION

Jazzy, Scott's Buddy

Doggie Devos is dedicated to my husband, Scott Covington.
What a preacher!
What a husband!
What a dog lover!
What a friend!

Thank you, Scott, for being an amazing man of God whose walk of faith is marked by kindness, integrity, determination, and passion for the Lord and others! Oh yes, and doggies too!

Table of Contents

1 Do You Need a Bark Collar? - Danika Deva   01

2 Duke's Eyes of Love - Susan Fitzgerald   07

3 It Just Happens - Sherry McClurkin   13

4 If I Only Had a Dog! - Yvette Perrin   21

5 Joey - Our Gift from God - Kathy Jo Kahn   29

6 God Saved Them Both - Linda Snyder   36

7 The Good Shepherd - Kathy Gifford   41

8 Heidi's Golden - Michelle Pitsenbuger   49

9 My Journey with Brownie - Sybil Fariss Nicely   53

10 The One-Eyed Blind Dog - Danika Deva   59

11 Overnight Healing - Tomi Woodward   63

12 Holly - Our Protector - Scott Covington   69

13 Waiting on "Paws" - Danika Deva   75

14 Revel in the Heartache - Sherry McClurkin   81

15 God's Gift to Me and My Gift to God - Lorriane H. Conklin   87

16 What Fifi Taught Me About the Lord - Heather Hart   95

17 Draw Close to Me - Danika Deva   101

ACKNOWLEDGEMENTS

We would like to thank Heather Hart for creating a spectacular cover design, Niki Banning for tremendous editing, and Kathy Gifford for fabulous format revisions.

What a blessing you all are to our contributors and our readers!

FORWARD

Photo Credit: Kelsey Kahn

Do you love Doggies? Do you want to see how they have changed the lives of many and made an impact in how they now love the world? If so, read on and enjoy Doggie Devos: Taking "Paws" to Reflect on God's Goodness.

As you can see picture, Joey is reading too! You will read his story later on in the book.

A BIG THANKS

A big thanks to Sonya Weaver for her phenomenal photos throughout this book (except the ones connected to each author)! Sonya is a professional photographer that specializes in photographing animals. She and her husband reside on their farm in Central Virginia, where they have an assortment of animals, most of which have landed there for rescue from bad circumstances. Along with her artwork, photography, and caring for their farm, she and her dear friend, Beth, have started an organization (SWAG ~ Southern Welfare Animal Group) to help the animals of the Charlotte County Shelter, as well as lending a hand with the counties around them.

The photos herein are of rescue dogs that have come from various less-than-wonderful situations but that are now living their best lives in the homes of people who love them.

https://www.facebook.com/profile.php?id=100091128134722

1 Do You Need a Bark Collar?

Danika Deva

Lacy not only likes to bark, but she likes to play in the clay-filled dirt of Virginia.

Recently my dog, Lacy, started barking at everything, and I mean everything. You name it: a bird, cat, firefly, an airplane, a spider, a dog walking by with the owner, and on and on. You get the picture.

Although we do want dogs to bark to warn us about something or someone, we don't want them to bark continually so the neighbors begin to complain.

One day, I found a bark collar at a garage sale (yeah, God!) and put it on her. She quickly learned to selectively bark. She gets three barks, then there is a small zap. Some of you might say this is not kind to the dog, but my plan is to take it off of her in a week or less. She must learn that barking at nothing is not productive. It should be only to alert or warn us.

Not even 24 hours later, she has learned her lesson and has stopped barking. Wow, what peace we have in our yard, and I bet the neighbors are happy, too. I know I am!

While I was gathering wood for my woodstove, I was thinking about how quickly Lacy learned this. I thought about our homes and how we, as parents, need to put our bark collars on. We don't need to nag and yak about everything, but focus on the things that our children need a warning about. We should alert them, not bark, bark, bark at them!

Now, I don't think any of us are going to run out and buy a bark collar to stop yapping at those around us, but we might ask God where we have been barking lately and ask for His help to quit. With God's help, we can stop yipping at our spouse, our siblings, or those around us. As with my dog, our kids and spouses won't listen if we continually bark. They will just get annoyed, just like my neighbors. Annoyance doesn't build community, it builds division and more complaining.

Today, let's commit to even go a step further and speak words that build and encourage, instead of yakking, nagging, barking, or grunting.

Don't use foul or abusive language. Let everything you say
be good and helpful, so that your words will be an
encouragement to those who hear them.
Ephesians 4:29 NLT

Prayer Moment:
Lord, it is only with your help that I can stop barking and start blessing. Guide my words to be words of warning and encouragement to those who hear them. Remind me of this so that I can build community in my family and friends.

Danika is a Jesus-loving, intentionally-living, principality-fighting, woman of God who delights in coaching others in the areas of business, hope and life. As an educator and hope dealer, she offers simple, life-changing solutions through her writing, speaking, and coaching.

"I promise didn't bark."

Her God-given Ph.D. in "Hard Knocks" and "God Rocks" has equipped her to inspire others to "Be Intentional," and lean into Jesus in hardship so they can heal and flourish with HOPE.
She can be found at DanikaDeva.com.

2 Duke's Eyes of Love

Susan Fitzgerald

It was his 12-week-old light blue puppy eyes that first grabbed my heart when Duaine, my husband, and our granddaughters arrived on a farm to pick up our newest family member. He was a yellow Labrador Retriever pup, and we named him Duke. Little did we know what was in store for us in the next two years. We took on the tasks of raising a puppy: house breaking, leash training, all the things a puppy requires. In addition to incorporating Duke into our family, I was also busy caring for my aging parents and working my part-time job as a real estate paralegal, as well as juggling household manager duties for Duaine and me.

In April 2019, our world exploded. I suffered a massive brain bleed and was paralyzed on my left side. I went from being an active, self-sufficient 66-year-old woman, to relying on others for even the simplest of self-care tasks. During the next 10 weeks of hospitalization and intensive inpatient rehabilitation, I slowly began relearning how to sit upright, stand, and walk with a cane. During that time, my husband, daughter, and son visited as often as they could and occasionally Duke accompanied my husband. By now, Duke was a full-grown adult dog weighing over 90 pounds. The sounds and smells of a busy medical facility brought back many of his puppy tendencies to react immediately and think later!

In June 2019, I came home to my new reality. God had been my constant source of hope during my acute illness and rehabilitation, and my go-to song of comfort and peace was "Turn Your Eyes Upon Jesus," sung by Lauren Daigle. Duke and I spent a lot of time together during those early days back home. He rarely left my side. He would often stand or sit in front of me and stare into my eyes with his beautiful goldish-brown eyes full of love (he had long outgrown those puppy blue eyes). It was as if he was trying to see deep into my soul. It struck me that this was how God's eyes of love search my soul. What a comfort that was then, and still is to me!

Duke and I still spend many of our days together, often staring lovingly into each other's eyes. God knew exactly when to bring this precious dog we call Duke into my life, and I thank Him every day for that!

We know it so well, we've embraced it heart and soul,
this love that comes from God. God is love. When we
take up permanent residence in a life of love,
we live in God and God lives in us.
1 John 4:16 MSG

Prayer Moment:
God, thank you for your perfect love and your perfect timing,
and thank you especially for our precious dogs. Amen.

Susan Fitzgerald is a retired Real Estate paralegal from Heslep & Kearney P.C., a Lexington VA Law firm. A proud graduate of James Madison University, she was inspired to pursue a career in Clinical Laboratory Science. She worked in this capacity for 26 years, after which she embarked on a totally different career path to allow more time to spend with her family.

3 It Just Happens

Sherry McClurkin

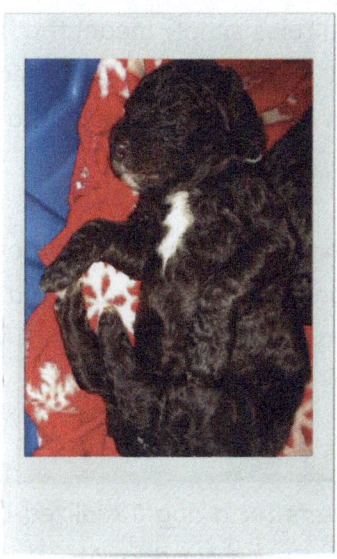

I love cats. I have had them for decades. Since my childhood, really. I also have a way of thinking that says, "Ok, I've conquered that. What's the next challenge?" which would explain my entire decision-making process when I decided to get a dog. I've had cats, I know how to raise cats, so it's time for something new. "Hey, let's get a dog," I thought to myself.

At the time, I was renting a condo with my two cats. I wanted to do the right thing, so I checked with the condo owner and the board to see if there was a limit on pets. Adding a dog would bring the number to three pets, plus me. I found out the owner and board had changed the rules to make the condo units pet-free but had grandfathered me in, which meant the cats could stay - but I couldn't get a dog.

13

This brings me to another mindset I get into: dealing with rules. I don't like rules that seem arbitrary or cause me problems, so I'll either ignore them or find a way around them. This gets me into plenty of trouble, but that's another story. Finding out I couldn't add a dog due to someone else's rules simply meant that it was time to move. Actually, it meant more than moving. It meant it was time for me to buy my own house, so I'm the one to make the rules.

Fast forward several months, and I bought a beautiful house at much lower cost than I ever thought I'd qualify for and in a lovely neighborhood with trails and wonderful green spaces. It was a dream come true, a perfect home for a dog I dreamed of owning. It all felt so God-given.

As I looked through rescue shelters for a dog, I realized I knew nothing, absolutely nothing, about raising a dog. Also, I had no items to care for a dog: no crate, no bed, no bowls, no leash, nothing. I was overwhelmed. I knew I couldn't simply go get any of those necessary items without knowing the size and other details about the dog. I was in a stalemate and didn't know what to do.

Then I saw an ad for puppies, gorgeous 2-week-old puppies with photos. They were Labradoodles, which was a much sought after mix for their intelligence, beautiful coat, and fun-loving temperament. I was in cuteness overload! My brilliant logic then shifted to say go with a puppy (which I had never had before).

It made perfect sense to me, and everything seemed to fall neatly into place. It all just happened. It helped that the breeder had a good reputation, lived nearby, and wanted owners to visit the puppies as often as possible once they reached four weeks old. I visited my chosen puppy every week, and I have photos of me holding that sweet baby at four-weeks, five-weeks, six-weeks, and seven-weeks—the week I finally got to bring her home. And she changed my life. I deeply believe my sweet Labradoodle named Reesie is a gift from God who came into my life at just the right time.

Christ changed my life, too, and in ways I never imagined. I had no concept of Christ growing up, just as I had no concept of raising a dog. Christ came into my life in His timing and His manner; it was no earlier than I needed and no later. God changed my relationships, my self-view, and whom I consider my community. Reesie did all those things, too. I never knew a dog could do that. Christ grew me, and He continues to push me to be better and more Christ-like, which is an ongoing process. I feel that with Reesie, too. I push myself to be better with her: a better handler, giving her better care such as the type of food and vet I choose, and building a life that grows and pushes her in ways she enjoys.

I took Reesie to work with me when she reached 10-weeks-old, and that continued until we moved out-of-state almost three years later. My clients loved that Reesie was in my office with us. She touched their lives, not just mine. And that's exactly what Christ does. He touches the lives of those around me because Holy Spirit resides in me. It just happens.

I don't have to do anything to make it happen. It's part of the package of accepting Christ as my Lord and Savior. My life is no longer mine (not that it was in the first place!). The difference is I accept that my life is no longer mine, and I freely hand my life over to the one who gave me life in the first place: Christ.

Looking back, I was scared to get a dog because I felt I wouldn't know how to raise her. Yet, something kept pushing me forward, and I trusted in my ability to figure things out. Reesie was not scared to come home with me, she simply trusted in me. She's not scared to rely on me, but she believes I am going to take loving care of her.

That's what it's like to give ourselves over to Christ. We choose to trust and stop trying to figure it all out on our own. We choose to accept that there's much more to this life and this world than we can ever know. And we choose to acknowledge there is a God who does know all, loves us as we are, wants more and better for us, and will help us get there.

If you have not yet accepted Jesus Christ as your Lord and Savior, then I invite you to do so now. If you have accepted Jesus Christ as your Lord and Savior, then I invite you to deepen that relationship now.

"For I know the plans I have for you," declares the Lord,
"plans to prosper you and not to harm, plans to give you
hope and a future."
Jeremiah 29:11 NIV

Prayer Moment:

Dearest Loving Heavenly Father, you are so far beyond our comprehension, yet you gave us your one and only Son in the form of Jesus Christ, to walk among us and demonstrate to us Your true love of us which included the ultimate sacrifice of Jesus's human life, to cover our sins. I could never do enough to cover my own sins, let alone anyone else's. None of us can, but Jesus could and He did, because He was unblemished and both fully human and fully God. I accept and believe in these truths. I freely invite you into my heart and my life. You are the one true God. There is no other, and all I have is Yours. I humbly give myself to you in whole and I will follow You, no one else, for the rest of my days. Amen.

Sherry McClurkin is an Emotional Balance Expert & Webinar Instructor with her company, Rebellious Emotional Balance. Her focus is to share & teach her practical and comprehensive steps for lasting emotional balance via live webinars. Sherry teaches and demonstrates simple, proven, brain-science based methods that train the brain to default to calm, confident, focused, and empowered. While the webinars are in a coaching format, Sherry brings her extensive history as a Trauma Therapist of over 10 years into her webinars. She's also a Certified Trauma Specialist. Sherry's proudest achievement is as a dog mom to 2 dogs. One is a smart, sassy, curly-haired Labradoodle who achieved the AKC's Good Citizen Certificate and a 2nd-level trick dog certification. The other is a sweet, young dog, newer to Sherry's pack, so the training is in the early stages. Sherry believes dogs and humans alike need to constantly train their brains.

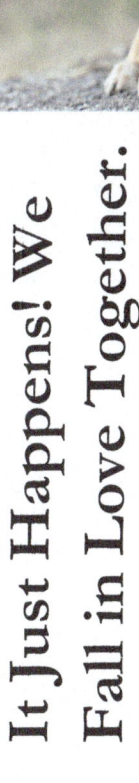

It Just Happens! We Fall in Love Together.

4 If I Only Had a Dog!

Yvette Perrin

Like all children, my son, Sean, wanted a dog. At the time, we were living a military life, so we had always hesitated to get a dog. Our lives were busy. I questioned the responsibility, and I wondered how fair it would be to leave a dog alone from time to time, due to our busy lifestyle.

One day I was opening the refrigerator, and behind me, my son was talking to himself. I heard him say, "Oh, if I only had a dog!" I felt it in my heart.

A few days later, I hosted a Tupperware party in my home. Many ladies came, and some brought friends. Afterwards, one of the ladies said she could not stay for refreshments because she had to get back. She was a dog breeder and had some new Chihuahua puppies in need of her attention at home. She explained that some people were coming to buy a puppy that very night. Kiddingly, I said, "What a terrible thing to have to leave for!"

She said, "No, I really need to go. One of the dogs is crippled, and I must go check on him." She told me she would probably have to keep him, because no one would want a crippled dog. I asked her if the dog knew he was crippled. She said he did not! She told me he would squat like a girl dog and was able to get around just fine.

I made a decision right there. I told her I had just bought our homeschool supplies, so my budget was tight. But, if she would give me a few weeks, I wanted to buy that crippled dog.

At the time we decided to get our dog, Sean and I just so happened to be studying King David as part of his homeschool curriculum. In the book of 2 Samuel, history tells us that King David was a shepherd's son and tended sheep. God used David to speak peace to King Saul's soul. David was taken from the fields to serve the king, and he grew up in the palace.

He became so jealous of David that eventually, the king wanted David dead. War broke out, and in the end, King Saul fell on his sword and his son, Jonathan, died as well.

Despite the circumstances with King Saul, David and Jonathan had always remained friends. They were as close as brothers. They made promises to each other when the war broke out that if something happened to either one, they would take care of each other's family. When the war ended, as promised, David searched throughout the kingdom to see if anyone in the household of Saul was left. The only one was Mephibosheth, Jonathan's son.

Mephibosheth was just a baby when the war broke out. To protect him, the nursemaid who cared for Mephibosheth ran with him during a battle. She dropped him, and he became crippled. The war went on for some time, so by the time the war had ended, Mephibosheth had grown up. When David's men came to get him, I am sure he was frightened! In those times, culturally, if you were a family of the enemy, you were sentenced to death, but David wanted to honor his commitment to Jonathan.

David brought Mephibosheth into his court, dressed him in fine clothes, restored to him what belonged to his family, and sat him at the King's table. He sat in a position of honor. When Mephibosheth sat at the table, no one knew he was crippled.

Now, back to my little dog. The next day, Sean and I ran a few errands. When we got home, there was a message on my answering machine. The breeder said she thought that anyone who would take a dog—knowing he was crippled and had not seen him—should have the dog. Imagine the excitement Sean had! We were eager to bring our new puppy home. We named him Mephibosheth.

We were blessed to have Mephibosheth for nine years. During that time, God taught us so much about love through that little six-pound pup. He was faithful to our family. He stood up for us with other big dogs, he nestled us when were ill, he demanded we pay attention to him when he needed care, and always gave us love no matter if the house was clean, if our day was good, or if our day was bad. He was always there.

Through that experience, God taught our family to be more concerned about each other than we were about ourselves, to give more than we could ever get in return, and to love no matter what the day brings or does not bring. And the biggest lesson of all—that God is with us and for us!

The day Mephibosheth passed, I was grief stricken. I cried all night and have not had a dog since. The pain was too great! But I often think of Mephibosheth and the love that he gave to me and our family. I miss him and am thankful God allowed us the opportunity to experience such a great love. He is there!

The faithful love of the Lord never ends!
His mercies never cease.
Great is his faithfulness;
his mercies begin afresh each morning.
Lamentations 3:22-23 NLT

Prayer Moment:
Father, as I remember the blessing of Mephibosheth, I thank you for being the God of all creation and what a joy it is that you share your creation with all of humanity. Help me to be a caring and kind person to my family, my neighbors, and my friends. May I be faithful to You and Your Kingdom.
In the name of Jesus, Amen

Yvette Perrin has served the USA as an Air Force wife for over 26 years. Retiring in 2011, Yvette resides in the state of VA. She recently opened MiPa's Table Restaurant in Pamplin, VA, where she welcomes people to "Taste and See" that the Lord is good, while eating farm to table cuisine. She is a writer, grandmother of three, lover of all things ocean, and serves in her local community church.

Woof!

5 Joey – Our Gift from God

Kathy Jo Kahn

March 24, 2010

Today was not a fun day. Today, my brother and I woke up in a shelter, covered with scars. There were strangers all around, and I was so confused. How did we get here? Why does my body hurt? Why can't I be with my family? Why did my owner have to hurt us? All we did was try to love him and behave. I can hear my brother in the kennel across the way, howling for me. I try to howl back, but I don't think he can hear me. Everywhere around me is just barking and meowing, Barking, meowing, barking. Oh please, someone make it stop! There's so much noise, I can't even think.

Ooh, someone's coming. Maybe they will tell me what's happening. Hey (bark!) what is this place? Who are you? Where am I? HELP ME PLEASE! (Bark.. Bark.. BARK!!)

I keep thinking about my owner. I am sure they didn't mean to hurt me. It was an accident! If I had come when I was called, maybe he wouldn't have put those ropes on my feet and kicked me into the woodpile. I cut my head, but it was healing. My brother licked it clean for me, and I licked his wounds clean for him. Maybe if my brother would have behaved, I wouldn't have been blamed. He chased the cat, but I was chasing the mouse to help. I love catching mice, but I don't like cats. Never have. I was trying to eat the food my brother spilled so he wouldn't get caught, but that didn't turn out so well either. It was nice to have a full belly, but my brother didn't get food for two days. And my cheek sure hurt from the stick my owner used. If I apply what I have learned, I think I'd better behave here. I will just stay quiet, won't cause any trouble, and maybe these people won't hurt me. I will act like a gift and hopefully they will feed me and give me baths and talk to me. I just hope nobody yells or hits me anymore.

April 1, 2010

It's been a few weeks, and it's not so bad here. They use a lot of whiny voices and smile and try to play with me, but I prefer the corner of my room, under the blanket. I wish they would just feed me and leave me alone. It's not like I want to love them back. Love hurts!

Here she comes. She wants me to go for a walk again. Wag my tail, look 'em in the eyes, get my treat. Yummy! Today I pulled really hard when we walked by my brother and they stopped so I could say hello to him! As of this moment, I am gonna do everything I can to make people happy and try to get outta here. I see so many others being greeted by new families, and it looks like the happy ones get to go and the mean ones are still here.

I am gonna try looking happier and maybe one day, I will get "the gift" of a new home, a new family, and a chance to love and protect them.

April 24, 2010
Today my brother and I were put in a car and placed in our new homes. I am scared and I am sad. We didn't get to go to the same family. I barked my goodbye and cried quietly in the lap of this strange girl. She was nice and kept saying, "It's gonna be okay! You are our special gift!"

August 11, 2023
It's been three wonderful years with this family, and today I will take my last breath. I feel them petting me and holding my feet gently, and I hear them crying and telling me and the doctor what a gift from God I was. I wish I could show them with a tail wag or a cute smile how much I love them, but I am on my way to a new home now. From what I can see, it looks like a really beautiful place.

As you can tell, that was a brief summary of what the first three months were like for our beloved four-legged family member, soul-healer, and precious gift for our family, as well as her final day with us. We thought we were rescuing her, but instead she spent her whole life, to her last joyous playtime in the backyard, doing everything she could to make sure that we felt love, joy, peace, and comfort. Joey was the best representative of the unconditional love the Father has for us that I have ever experienced. From the look in her eye, to the smile she would make with her lips, the nuzzle of trust that you had to earn, and her constant bark to warn us of potential danger, Joey was unconditional love.

Over time, we figured out that the person who hurt her was an older man who wore a baseball cap and smoked. There was a ferocity of barking and a lunging response to certain people that even after 12 years of comfort, care, safety and love, nothing overcame her trauma and memories of whomever hurt her. Those scars were deep and ugly, and she was determined to never let that person or anyone like them near us. She became our beloved gift.

My dear brothers and sisters, do not be fooled about this.
Every good action and every perfect gift is from God.
These good gifts come down from the Creator of the sun, moon, and stars, who does not change like their shifting shadows.
God decided to give us life through the word of truth so we might be the most important of all the things he made.
James 1:16-18 NCV

Prayer Moment:
Dear Father in heaven, Thank you for the gift of your sacrifice, your faith, your kindness, your love, your compassion, your wisdom, your peace, and your comfort in our time of need. Your gift of unconditional love and unexpected intervention is around me every day. Help me to recognize your generosity, your providence, protection, opportunities, and your relentless pursuit for me. Show me how to be a gift to others in small ways, even when they are not ready to see Your presence, so in abundant ways when Your people cry out in their time of need, asking for healing or a miracle, they will know there is no greater name to call upon then Jesus.

Kathy Jo Kahn is a proud alumnus of Northwest University's Creatio Audio Engineering Program with a BA in Music. She holds a Master's Certificate in Music Business from Berklee Online School of Music, and is the proud recipient of NYU's On-line TISCH School Certificate from the Clive Davis School of Music Business & Technology. As a pastor, worship leader, and recording artist, God has used her to help trauma survivors and those in recovery. In music, God has called her to "Gather the sound of the coming King," so she is always listening for the frequency of our Father's voice as she watches for God's artistic creations and servant leaders who seem to have a similar passion for building His Ecclesia, God's church.

In 2019, Kathy Jo launched a 501(c)(3) non-profit organization, Summit Heritage Alliance, a ministry department of Artists in Christian Testimony, International, which is dedicated to building community through outreach and a passion for creativity. She is an Ordained "Ecclesia" Pastor through United New Testament International, Founder of Rock The Church Northwest, Director of Worship Arts for Veterans for Worship, Worship Pastor at The Fairview Church in Seattle, Director/Producer of Nativity Story by Candlelight, and a Christian recording artist and leader of Tears of Praise Worship Band. She is currently working on her 3rd CD and planning to launch her own recording company in 2024, Thirsty Willow Studios.

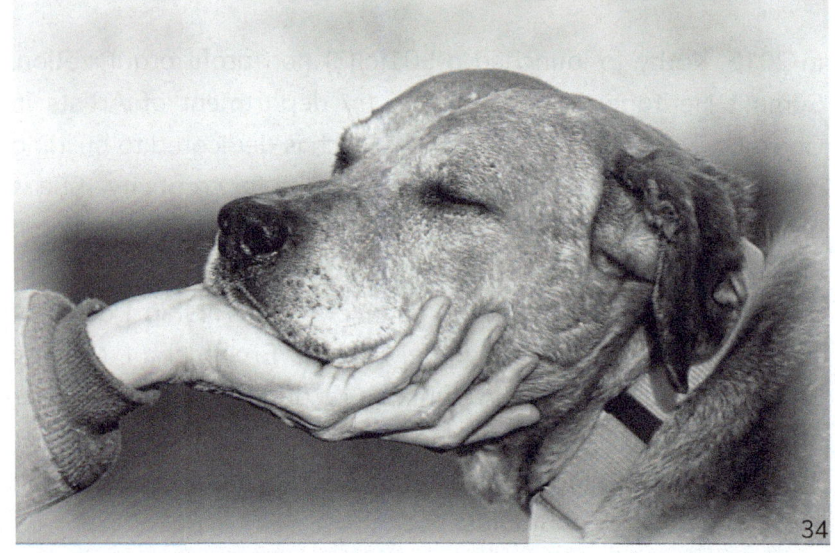

6 God Saved Them Both

Linda Snyder

Bill, Schnoodle, and Elvis

My husband, Bill, had a stroke in May 2013. For the first year, he struggled to do the most basic things. Family members came in to help with whatever we needed. While I had to go to work to keep us going, he spent a fair bit of time alone, sitting by himself, watching TV, and feeling useless. His world had changed and he didn't know what to do or how to handle it. He was sad, scared, and overwhelmed. What good was he now? How was he supposed to contribute and provide for his family?

While I still had a job to go to, chores to do, and errands to run - Bill didn't. He needed to feel useful. He needed purpose. He needed a friend.

God sent "Emmy."

We found Emmy (affectionately known as "Schnoodle") very near our home. She was owned by a Chihuahua breeder, but she could not have puppies. What good was she now? How was she supposed to contribute and earn her keep? When we went to pick her up, she was surrounded by puppies doing their puppy thing; romping, playing, and competing for attention. Emmy, however, was cowering in a corner looking sad, scared, and overwhelmed. The man picked her up and handed her to Bill. It was love at first sight—at least for him.

It took Schnoodle another day to figure out she was finally home. But once she did, Schnoodle and Bill were inseparable. God had given Bill a purpose: to love, protect, and adore this sweet, beautiful dog.

God gives us what we need when we need it. Bill needed to feel useful and needed again. Schnoodle needed a forever home where someone loved her unconditionally and took care of her every need. They were a match made in heaven.

And my God shall supply all your needs according to His riches in glory by Christ Jesus. Now to our God and Father be glory forever and ever. Amen.
Philippians 4:19-20 NKJV

Prayer Moment:

Dear Lord, Thank you for coming and saving us just when we need you. You know our thoughts, hearts, problems etc., and your timing is always best. Help us to turn to you during the tough times and watch you show up. In Jesus Name, Amen

Schnoodle

Linda Snyder lives in the tiny town of Chase City, Virginia. She loves serving God, baking cookies, and eating Mexican food. She and her husband Bill started an eBay store on July 4, 2023 and have been hustling and bustling ever since! Current furbabies include Baba the beagle, Migsy the Chihuahua, Furrbutt the orange long-haired tabby, and Cyber and Nettie, the one-eyed mama cat and her baby boy that just wandered up and stayed; plus any stray cat that needs a meal and wanders over at feeding time. Her favorite scripture is Jeremiah 29:11: "For I know the plans I have for you," declares the LORD, "plans to prosper you and not to harm you, plans to give you hope and a future." Isn't that cool! So don't worry, God's got your back!

Here I am, Pick Me!

7 The Good Shepherd

By Kathy Owen Gifford

Rocky (passed), Ozzie (passed), & Peanut.

Currently we have three dogs, all of whom are rescues. Peanut is a registered Miniature Poodle, weighing 16 pounds and is 17 years old. Milo is a 45 pound Australian Shepherd who is probably around age six. We've had him for four years. Charlie Tucker is an Aussie Doodle who weighs around 45 pounds and is still acts like a puppy at about 18 months. He's been with us since the end of April 2023.

Our dog Peanut is a gem! He used to be a beautiful boy, but now he looks a little rough. He still bosses the other dogs around, and is our darling, cranky old man. Our dog Milo is an amazing dog. He looks to us for guidance and is as obedient off-leash as on. Charlie Tucker is a crazy puppy-ish giant with energy to spare. He has a pretty great off button in that he stops (most of the time!) and sleeps super hard like puppies do.

A while back, I noticed Milo standing at a distance, herding Charlie, then standing at a distance again as Charlie ran around like crazy, just for fun. This is typical Australian Shepherd behavior with sheep. I think we've all seen the reels where the sheep are crammed into a fenced area and the Aussie or Border Collie runs on top of the herd's backs to find the clog and get the sheep running through again. These dogs are amazing! Our dog Milo came to us fairly untrained, and I don't think he's ever even seen sheep.

We can tell when Charlie has too much energy and needs to run around, so I tell them to "get outside" and "go get a job." He and Milo happily bolt out the dog door, and I follow. I direct Milo to "make him go!" and Milo sometimes chases. Many times he tells Charlie to "go!" and off goes Charlie, running around like crazy and getting some energy out. It's hilarious! (And soon you'll be able to watch the antics on my website!)

It got me thinking about our Good Shepherd. How many times do we need to run away from temptation, sin, some place we don't belong, or some attitude we need to shed? Sometimes we just need to go! Flee!

2 Timothy 2:22-24 (CEV) says, "Run from temptations that capture young people. Always do the right thing. Be faithful, loving, and easy to get along with. Worship with people whose hearts are pure. Stay away from stupid and senseless arguments. These only lead to trouble, and God's servants must not be troublemakers. They must be kind to everyone, and they must be good teachers and very patient."

Who is shepherding you? Is your shepherd following the Lord? Who are you shepherding? Are you following the Lord, dear leader?

Milo is a good leader because he was made to lead. He is a shepherd. When Charlie doesn't follow Milo's lead in the house when it's time to chill, Milo takes him out back for a run, resets his brain, and Charlie is happier for it. The first day I went out and directed Milo, I thought of how many times we as individuals go it alone, forget to plug into our leader, our Loving Father, Jesus, our own Good Shepherd, and the sweet Holy Spirit who lives within us.

Milo was effective on his own, leading Charlie; he was born to do it. But with me guiding him, he has learned when it is really necessary and he enjoys it so much because I get to tell him what a great guy he is and how proud I am of him. He gets to lean on me (figuratively and literally) as we watch Charlie Tucker run his crazy out together. It's delightful! Imagine how much the Father loves when we lean into Him. Imagine how delighted He is to see us doing His will.

He delights in us. "He brought me out to a spacious place; he rescued me because he delighted in me." Psalm 18:19 CSB

Did you know that "every good and perfect gift" comes from God, whether you know Him or not? "Every good and perfect gift is from above, coming down from the Father of lights, who does not change like shifting shadows." James 1:17 CSB. We consider our delightful dogs a gift from God, and we are reminded how God delights in us by seeing our own delight for them.

The next time I need the crazy run out of me (or one of my followers does), I'm going to remember Milo. For myself and those who follow me, I'm going to get away from temptation, run to the Father, seek Him for direction, and plug back in. "But seek first the kingdom of God and his righteousness, and all these things will be provided for you." Matthew 6:33 CSB

Are you plugged in? Who's leading you? Who's following you? Who are you leading? Have you surrounded yourself with too many earthly leaders, or do you need to be led more by the Holy Spirit? Have you invited God into your life? Have you cried out for help and forgiveness? Do it today. Today is the Day of Salvation!

For more reading, please open your Bible and read Psalm 23 again as if for the first time. He really loves us, and He shepherds us well.

*But seek first the kingdom of God and his righteousness,
and all these things will be provided for you.*
Matthew 6:33 CSB

Prayer Moment:
Lord, I realize you are
God and I'm not.
Please forgive me and
come into my life.
Guide and direct me
every second of the
day. In Jesus' Name,
Amen

Charlie Tucker   Charlie Tucker and Milo

Kathy Owen Gifford lives in north Alabama, is a former desktop publisher and teacher who currently is a stay at home wife and caregiver of husband Stephen, mother-in-law Rae, and three spoiled rotten, wild dawgs. The eldest of five children, she was raised in a Christian home on the missionary field in Costa Rica and Guatemala, and loves Jesus! She and Stephen are proud aunt and uncle to 17 nieces and nephews, two nieces-in-law, one darling great-niece and two precious great-nephews. A proud graduate of Samford University, Kathy obtained her BA in 1998, and then her M. Ed. in Design Technology for Learning at University of West Alabama in 2020. A lifelong learner, Kathy is trying to finish reading 50 books this year, tackle sourdough bread, and learn how to groom Charlie Tucker. You can see more about Kathy at www.kathygifford.solutions or on Facebook at Kathy Owen Gifford-Also.

I found a home!

8 Heidi's Golden

Michelle Pitsenbarger

Dexter taking a snooze!

When my husband got transferred to West Virginia, it meant my four children and I had to leave our friends behind. The move was hard emotionally and physically for all of us, and I was so lonely.

At the new house, when I would cut the grass, a golden retriever would show up in my yard. He would climb on the deck of the zero-turn mower when the blade was disengaged and "I swear" the dog would hug me. I could not believe it, but it continued to happen time after time, and I believe God sent me grace through that dog. After many times of Dexter climbing on the mower with me, the family who owned him allowed him to come live with us. Our family received grace just by being together with Dexter.

After a time, we moved to Tennessee, and of course, Dexter came with us. My daughter, Heidi, and I used to fuss (in fun, of course!) over whose dog Dexter was. But as I watched him get older and slower and start losing his hearing, I stopped fussing, let her "have" him, and gave her grace to prepare for the end of his life.

One day, Heidi told me, "Mom, Dexter will outlive me." The sad truth was that, unbelievably, he did outlive her, as she was killed a month later. Now, six months after the loss of my fun-loving daughter, I give Dexter all the grace that an old dog needs. He was loved so much by my girl and he is now my dog. I will care for him until his end days and bless his days as he blessed our lives all those years.

The Lord will increase his graces toward you, even toward you, and toward your children. Ye are blessed of the Lord, which made the heaven and the earth. The heavens, even the heavens are the Lord's: but he hath given the earth to the sons of men. The dead praise not the Lord, neither any that go down into the place of silence. But we will praise the Lord from henceforth and forever. Praise ye the Lord.
Psalm 115:14-18 GNV

Prayer Moment:
Lord, thank you for the grace that you give us everyday. Thank you that you can use our dog to show us Grace and give us LOVE at just the right time. Our hearts are grateful for your furry, huggable gifts to us. In Jesus' name, Amen.

Michelle Pitsenbarger, along with her husband Kevin, are farm owners. She loves people, dogs, and now goats and chickens. She is an instructor in junior high and high school and resides in East Tennessee.

Get it, Girlies!

9 My Journey with Brownie

Sybil Fariss Nicely

Brownie

I am currently facing a challenge where I am having to search my long-term memory. I was raised on a one-hundred-acre working farm in lower Campbell County, VA, with lots of animals: cows to milk, pigs to feed, horses to ride and plow the fields, chickens to feed and harvest the eggs, and dogs and cats to pet and play with all day. The crops consisted of corn to eat and dry feed for the cattle and pigs including the stalks, wheat to be thrashed and taken to the mill to be ground for flour for hot biscuits, and soybeans and hay to be baled for food for the livestock during the winter months.

We had a huge garden of vegetables and melons for canning for use during the winter, and tobacco to harvest and be taken to the market for income for our family.

This was of a different era than today, one of no running water or indoor bathroom. We lived in the home where my dad was born just after the turn of 1900. Our source of water was from a spring several hundred feet away. No appliances were electric except the refrigerator, so it was necessary to have the wood pile nearby to split and gather wood for the cookstove daily and to fuel the heaters during the cold season. Even though most of the families had many children, I only had one brother who was five years, five months, and five days older than me. Therefore, the fewer the children, the greater the number of chores and tasks for each child every day.

Most homes in the country were in the middle of the property, so there was an equal distance to go to work in the field, to harvest the crops, or care for the animals. Our home was just feet from the back border with our nearest neighbor, so we had to walk to the fields to work and tend. At times, we would take the tractor to cultivate the ground or the truck to the field to bring garden harvest back to the house to prepare for meals or can for later use.

I don't remember a time when we didn't have at least one dog. Our dogs were around us all the time that we were outside, following us wherever we were going or with us when we were working.

They warned us of people or unwanted animals coming near us while we were at the house or in the field. Mostly, they wanted our attention and our love and care, but they had certain things that they needed to do besides protecting us. They loved to herd the cows and corral any of the stray animals that may have worked their way out of their pasture or pen.

The first dog I remember having was Brownie, a golden retriever mixed with who knows what. He was a beautiful light-brownish color with long floppy ears. I've often wondered why my brother and I loved to pick his ears up and blow in them. He would always shake his head to get the air out. We'd even pull his ears up toward the top of his head with them overlapping each other. He loved to have his coat combed and brushed. He'd always be as gentle as could be, just happy to be with us and have our attention.

I wish I could remember all the circumstances and details around this particular day. It was getting late on that summer day and my mother called Brownie to come to her. I had often seen my mother call him and instruct him to do certain things. This particular day, the instruction was for Brownie to take me to the field to get my dad. She told Brownie that he needed to let me hold his ear and take me to find my dad. I've often wondered how Brownie knew which field my dad was working in that day, but away we went, with me holding tightly to his left ear. He slowed his fast pace to mine since I was just four years old. It was more than a quarter of a mile down the hill, across a brook, up a hill, through the cow pasture and orchard, across a branch, through a field, through a ravine, up a tall hill to where we reached my dad.

My mother believed and trusted that Brownie would take me, watch over me, keep me safe, and lead me to where she had instructed him to take me. How encouraging it is to us that we can not only believe in our Lord and Savior, but we can trust Him as He watches over us and keeps us safe as He leads us in the path He has for us. By trusting in Him, we are believing He will do for us what he says He will do. So how much more can we connect ourselves to our faithful Savior than anyone else? This teaches us that our Savior takes care of our every need. Praise the Lord!

Trust in the Lord with all your heart and lean not on
your own understanding.
Proverbs 3:5 NKJV

Prayer Moment:
Dear Lord, Thank you for guiding me in your path and giving me the light to follow. In Jesus' Name, AMEN! In Jesus' name, Amen

Sybil Fariss Nicely wrote her first required poem at the age of 11. It was received with high praise, which led to a lifetime hobby and pastime of haiku, poetry, and short stories on various subjects. She has written and given away far too many written pieces to count to new moms for birthdays, anniversaries, and thinking of you/just because/just for fun poetic pieces. She was first published in two local weekly newspapers, and in several of the National Book of Poetry volumes. She is currently working on chapters of her life stories in Story Worth for her family.

We love to play!

10 The One-Eyed Blind Dog

Danika Deva

Jinju gingeringly walking in the grass.

Jinju, my friend's one-eyed completely blind Shi-tzu, was staying with us for the weekend, and boy, did I learn a few things.

Jinju is a sweet, gentle, temperamental dog who often stays with our family while her owners go out of town.

Jinju, which means "pearl" in Korean, usually hangs out on the couch all day. Although she is blind, she jumps on and off the couch and 'occasionally' finds her potty pad. Other than that, her life is pretty devoted to just hanging out on the sofa.

When I take Jinju out in my yard to go potty, she gingerly walks around the grass to find just the right spot. When the perfect spot is found, she feverishly circles and circles, then does her business.

On the other hand, when I put her on a leash to take her on a walk, she becomes a new dog. No more hesitation, no more precautious pup, no more, "I'm afraid because I can't see." Once she's on the leash, she takes off down the road, traveling at the speed of light.

At first, I thought it was the road and her comfort traveling down it, since she often goes on walks with her owner. But then I realized that Jinju knew she was safe because she was attached to the leash. In fact, she was leading me on the walk. She was so confident. She knew the master (me, at the time) was connected to her. Even when we traveled on the grass, she seemed more self-assured and confident. Gone was the pearl of insecurity!

In reflection, I started to ask myself why I'm not more confident when I know, in fact, that I am connected to my Lord. Why do I gingerly attempt to do what He wants, yet lack the security to go where He leads? Why do I have the stubborn resistance of self? I, at times, am actually pulling on the leash in the other direction. What is that about, and why can't I be more like Jinju?

She is completely blind, yet her trust is greater than mine. She never resists, but keeps on cruising down the road, knowing that I won't purposely take her into any harm like a pricker-bush or a hole. In reality, she might accidentally fall in, but I would be there to help her and pull her out.

Isn't that how our precious Lord is? Life has many bushes and holes, and He is there to tend to our scratches and even pull us out.

HE IS THERE. He is there for each one of us. How thankful I am to be connected to God my Father. How comforting to know that I don't have to look around at all the distractions, but forge straight ahead in the plan that He has set for me.

What about you? Are you stubbornly resisting His guidance and direction? Or are you connected to Him, trusting that He will lead as you confidently walk ahead? Are you peacefully traveling down the middle of the street with freedom and God-assurance? It is only with God that we can have this security: His security. Let's follow Jinju's example. Let's trust Him today, and see where the road will take us!

I will instruct you and teach you in the way you should go;
I will counsel you with my eye upon you.
Psalm 32:8 ESV

Prayer Moment:
Dear Lord, Help me to leash up and confidently follow you, doing what you want me to do! I don't want to walk in trepidation or fear, but boldly obey, while tied to You. Thank you that I can trust You as you lead. In Jesus' name, Amen.

Picture Perfect

11 Overnight Healing

Tomi Woodward

Lovely Lauren

God healed my dog's back overnight! It was unbelievable, but it happened!

I got Lauren in 1985 when I lived in Warner Robins, Georgia. I went into the local mall's pet store and saw her. She was too big for the cage she was in. I told my husband at the time that he needed to go get his checkbook, because I wasn't leaving her there.

Lauren was a Cocker Spaniel and the most beautiful dog ever. She had long, silky, feathery hair on her legs and body. She was a light creamy tan color with a small white blaze on her nose and the biggest brown eyes that were so expressive and kind.

Lauren traveled with us when we moved to California in 1987, and she moved with me to North Carolina after my divorce. Then she moved with me after I remarried and moved to Virginia. She always knew somehow what I was feeling and was always attentive when I was crying or upset. We had both endured intense abuse, and because of that, she always knew how to console me.

One day, Lauren started having problems with her back and back legs. She couldn't walk and was whining and crying in pain when I touched her. I took her to three vets and the orthopedic vet said surgery was necessary to save her. That was a whopping $3,000 to $5,000, which I didn't have.

I brought her home, put her in her bed, and started praying, telling God that I did not have the money for an expensive surgery and she was too young to die. I got on my knees, laid hands on her, commanded all infirmity to leave her, and believed that she was healed in Jesus' name. The next morning, I got up for work, went downstairs to check on her—and she got up out of her bed like nothing was ever wrong. She was never sick another day until she passed in 2002.

May the Lord give you children—
you and your descendants!
May you be blessed by the Lord,
who made heaven and earth!
Heaven belongs to the Lord alone,
but he gave the earth to us humans.
The Lord is not praised by the dead,
by any who go down to the land of silence.
But we, the living, will give thanks to him
now and forever.
Psalm 115:14-18 GNV

Prayer Moment:
Lord, thank you for your healing touch. Thank you for using Lauren to remind us of your power. In Jesus' name, Amen.

Tomi Woodward currently lives in Rice, Virginia. She manages a concrete plant and is restarting her pet business named Pawsitive Love and Care Pet Sitting. She has had dogs and cats and small animals her whole life, and of course, she loves children too. Her greatest achievement was having her son at 34, and successfully raising him as a single mother. She has been a photographer, massage therapist, and a school bus and truck driver. She would like to someday own her own homestead and have kennels for pet-sitting and rescues, and would love to build tiny homes to take in homeless veterans and help them overcome challenges in life.

12 Holly – Our Protector

Scott Covington

Holly

We bought a Border Collie for my son, Josh. Holly was probably one of the best dogs I've ever been around. She was intelligent, and she was very loving and kind.

She was devoted to both my boys, Josh and Jared, and she felt it was her continual job to take care of them. As you know, being a Border Collie, that was her purpose. In fact, she wore a path around the trampoline, circling around it while they jumped, thinking she was herding them.

One time when the boys were climbing a tree, she actually managed to get eight feet off the ground by jumping onto a picnic table, onto a branch, and then climbing up the tree.

We learned of her devotion early as a young pup when we put her in a laundry room while the boys were outside. In a short amount of time, she scratched a hole completely through the door because she wanted to be near and protect the boys.

When she was older, we found that she was sick and had to have a very serious operation. The doctor said that she had the worst case of heartworms he had ever seen. We didn't realize that heartworms were extremely prevalent in our area and that she had gotten them.

After her surgery, we had to keep her secluded and in a quiet place, so we put her in one of the boys' bedrooms. When we came back in the house after the boys had played on the trampoline, we noticed that even though she had had surgery, Holly had torn the shades down in the bedroom trying to get to the boys on the trampoline. That was her job, being out there with the boys when they were outside, to hover over them and protect them, no matter how hurt or in need of healing she was.

The tenacity she showed in doing her task was not half-hearted or on and off, but it was full-blown and beautiful to see.

What task has God given you to do? Shouldn't we have that same tenacity in doing whatever God has called us to do?

*"So whether you eat or drink, or whatever you do,
do it all for the glory of God."
1 Corinthians. 10:31b NIV*

Prayer Moment:
Lord, help me to do the task you have given me with the joy, whole-heartedness and fullness of that little dog. In Jesus' name, Amen!

Scott Covington is a retired teacher and is currently serving as pastor of Buena Vista Baptist Church. He loves the breed of herding dogs and currently has an Australian Shepherd named Jazzy. You can read about Jazzy in the next chapter in this book.

13 Waiting on "Paws"

Danika Deva

"I see an SQ!!!," barked Jazzy!

As I was taking my dog for a walk today, she saw a squirrel. Of course being an Australian Shepherd, she had to go chase after it full-blast. In fact, we can't even say the word 'squirrel' at our house without her going crazy. We have to say 'SQ' or 'fluffy, long-tailed animal.'

As she was ready to chase the squirrel, I said, "No, Jazzy, no!" Why? Because I knew that my arm would be pulled out of socket and dislocated for life as she chased the squirrel. I had to help her change her mind so she wouldn't hurt me.

So it is with the enemy. He tries to get us distracted, discouraged, and detoured. However, we must stay the course, or we will get hurt. Sadly, we end up going down a road we don't want to, or we get off-course and struggle to get back on.

What helps us not chase the squirrels of life and get distracted by the enemy? God's Word, wise counsel from the people of God (community around us), and time in prayer with God. All those things help us stay focused and not chase the squirrels of life.

Additionally, taking "paws" (I mean pause) helps us. Too often, we see that SQ (thing, idea, purchase, job, activity) and want to take off like Jazzy, chasing SQ—but that doesn't serve us well. It just makes us confused about the next step.

God is there to guide us and help us make decisions. One of His names is "Gate," and He is the one that opens and shuts it for us, if we let Him.

Waiting on God is oh-so-hard at times, but in Psalms, we are told to wait expectantly on the Lord.

So, just how do we do that? To begin, we stop and don't chase the fluffy, long-tailed thing in front of us. We sit before the Lord and ask Him to show us what to do and where to go.

We surrender our life, repent for our sin, and wait (pause).

"When in doubt, don't!" is one of my favorite quotes. If we move forward in doubt, we end in a big pile of mess and then it's hard to get out. And yes, I am speaking from experience.

Another aspect of waiting is praising God while we wait. I have heard it said that "When God shuts a door, He always opens a window, but the halfway in between sure is long." Well, we need to be praising God in the hallway.

We need to make our plan, surrender it to God, look straight ahead, not get sidetracked by the SQs of life, and wait with praise until the Lord tells us what to do next. Let's not jump at everything before us and get wrapped up in things we shouldn't.

And remember, there are a whole lot of SQs out there, but only one loving God with a plan for you and your future!

> "Look straight ahead, and fix your eyes on what lies
> before you. Mark out a straight path for your feet; stay
> on the safe path. Don't get sidetracked; keep your feet
> from following evil."
> Proverbs 4:25-27 NLT

Prayer Moment:

Lord, help me to pause before you and wait for your guidance and direction. I don't want to run ahead in fear or carelessness. Thank you for being our guide and direction. In Jesus' name, Amen.

14 Revel in the Heartache

Sherry McClurkin

Rebel

I had the privilege of spending a year and three months loving a dog. Those 15 months turned out to be the final days of that young dog's life. I wanted a second dog as a companion for my other dog, almost like the new dog would be my dog's dog. No one knew that the new dog, whom I named Rebel, would die so soon. I haven't talked much about this experience, and only with a chosen few. It impacted me deeply.

Rebel had the sweetest face and was incredibly affectionate, most of the time. It was also a truly difficult year and three months. His death left me with great sadness, doubts, guilt, and what-ifs, along with relief and gratitude.

The hard times with Rebel were beautifully punctuated with precious moments. I am so grateful for those and how I can now remember him. If I knew in advance that Rebel would be so hard and die that soon, would I have taken him? I don't think so, because my plan was to have a lifelong, fun companion for my other dog, and then a built-in "replacement" when my other dog died of old age in another six or so years. That was my plan. God had a different plan.

God has plans for all of us. And we are generally unaware of them, often even oblivious. God may reveal bits and pieces, yet the overall plan is usually not ours to know. This is what happened with Rebel and me. I didn't know, and I'm glad I didn't know. We often think we want God to tell us in advance what's to come. The truth is that we can't handle it. We would focus on the heartache that is almost always part of God's plan, and we would miss the love, commitment, compassion, lessons, and all the other gifts God wraps into every plan for every one of us.

I can look back now and see how much I was loved and how much I learned through life with Rebel. I have far more understanding, compassion, and empathy for those who struggle with their dog and are doing everything possible to help their dog.

I take much more seriously what it means to have a rescue with their unique needs. I miss Rebel's level of affection and devotion to me.

I still want a second dog for my current dog. This experience, even with the pain has not dissuaded me from adding to my dog pack. Some people have a painful experience and then run away from anything seemingly like the experience so as not to have the heartache ever again. That's not what God wants for us. Imagine if God was like that about us. God would have given up on us in Genesis, with Noah and the flood. It would have been only a flood and no Noah, so that all humankind was wiped off the face of the Earth. God didn't do that, though. He wants our hearts open and loving even in the pain, just as God does with us. Jesus modeled love in the midst of great pain many times. Jesus used the analogy of a hen spreading her loving wings over her chicks to protect them. That's how much He wanted to protect us and also knew He couldn't. Jesus knew He would die on the cross for us and knew what He would go through to get to the cross. He knew some would still not believe He was truly the Son of God. That's pain; it was gut-wrenching, heart-breaking pain. And He did it anyway.

And God has given us his Spirit as proof that we live in him and he in us. Furthermore, we have seen with our own eyes and now testify that the Father sent his Son to be the Savior of the world. All who declare that Jesus is the Son of God have God living in them, and they live in God. We know how much God loves us, and we have put our trust in his love.

God is love, and all who live in love live in God, and God lives in them. And as we live in God, our love grows more perfect. So we will not be afraid on the day of judgment, but we can face him with confidence because we live like Jesus here in this world.

Such love has no fear, because perfect love expels all fear. If we are afraid, it is for fear of punishment, and this shows that we have not fully experienced his perfect love. We love each other because he loved us first.

1 John 4:13-19 NLT

Prayer Moment:

Dearest Loving Heavenly Father, may we never forget the extent to which You go to show us Your immense love for us. May we never forget that You loved us first, knowing the immense heartache we bring and cause. May we never forget that true, unconditional love includes pain; and pain allows the love, forgiveness, and blessings to shine ever brighter.

In Jesus's name, Amen.

15 God's Gift to Me, My Gift to God

Lorriane H. Conklin

Max

Max is an Australian Cattle Dog. He was up for adoption at Petco and I didn't even know it. I had to drive 30 miles to meet Max. My friend introduced us to the shelter and shared that all the dogs from there were chosen for adoption, except for Max. He was the only one not chosen, and probably because he was going to be a bigger dog.

Max has been with me for more than 10 years now. He was there when my husband, Harry, passed away, and during many ups and downs of life.

I tell my Max the weather report every morning before we have our daily prayers. If it's cold, I let him know that he needs a sweater, or if it's warm, I tell him that he can go out without it, and Max listens to me. Then, of course, on Sundays, we listen to Jonathan Fallwell's sermon, a great preacher just down the road. I just love his messages, and so does Max.

Because I can't drive, I can't work because of my health, and I can't get a job, I often think, "What is my purpose? God, what am I here for?"

And He always tells me, "Max needs you because right now he doesn't have anybody else."

And I say to myself, "It's a good thing I'm doing well, even after three strokes, a new heart valve at 87, several blood clots, falls, and currently, two kinds of cancer. If I passed away, who's gonna take Max? He is an old dog and has cataracts." One of my reasons for staying healthy is to care for that special dog. Even with two kinds of cancer, I do what I can to stay as healthy as possible by following a strict diet and monitoring it with the doctors.

In fact, when I wasn't even looking for someone to marry, God found someone for me. His friend introduced us and Harry and I were married over 50 years. In my heart, I had a description about him and he was everything I wanted and fit the bill.

When I am sad and miss Harry, I ask God to Help me. At those moments, Max comes over and comforts me. I know that is a special blessing from God.

And it's a funny thing. Two weeks ago, I thought about turkey for Thanksgiving and the people who celebrate Thanksgiving. Now, I usually have a hamburger or a hot dog, but I remember one Thanksgiving we had turkey. But this year, I wanted turkey and I looked up at the ceiling when I said, "God, I think I want Turkey." And you know what happened? Not even five minutes later my phone rings. It was Mom's Meals and they said, "We have turkey dinners. Would you like one?"

I ordered two and knew that God was listening. He listens a lot, even about the small things.

I'm so pleased that my life has been focused around God. As a youngster, my parents didn't go to church, but they made us go to a Catholic church where the service was always in Latin. All of the children would sit with a nun on each end of the pew to supervise us. We didn't have a Bible at home for some reason, but we were going to church.

My mother made a rule that if you didn't go to church, there would be no movies on Saturday. Since we wanted to see Roy Rogers and Gene Autry, we all went. We did have some church values and I did make my Holy Communion and I could make my commitment, but I didn't understand that I should read the Bible because it's God's word. And a true relationship with God comes from that. I knew about God, but I didn't really know Him in the true sense.

When I feel alone, I choose happiness because there are better places than where we are. A place of everlasting peace, joy, and no sorrow. It is Heaven. You have to believe in Jesus and that He died on the cross for us and our sin.

89

You have to commit your life to Him. It doesn't matter if you were a good person or not. God died for all. He died so we could have our sins taken away and go to Heaven with Him.

I have realized over the years that Max is for me to take care of and God, in the meantime, is taking care of me. I always tell Max that we are buddies and we take care of each other. That's beautiful.

If you openly declare that Jesus is Lord and believe in your heart that God raised him from the dead, you will be saved. For it is by believing in your heart that you are made right with God, and it is by openly declaring your faith that you are saved.

Romans 10:9-10 NLT

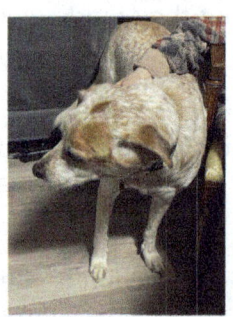

Prayer Moment: Lord, help us know that you are by our side, you never leave us, and you carry us through everything that happens to us. Thank you for your love.

Lorraine H. Conklin is a first-time author at the age of 88. She is an avid reader and dog lover. Her cheerful personality connects her with people. She resides in Rustburg, Virginia with Max, her precious dog, and fond memories of her late husband, Harry.

16 What Fifi Taught Me About Waiting for the Lord

Heather Hart

Fifi

A couple of months ago, we got a new puppy. However, when I say we got a new puppy, she's not really a puppy and she isn't really ours.

Let me explain. Fifi is just over a year old, and we got her for my mother-in-law, who's been hoping for a new dog for a while now. As much as my mother-in-law wanted a new dog, she isn't quite up to keeping Fifi around the clock yet. So, every morning we take Fifi over to my mother-in-law's house so she can keep her while my husband is at work and the kids are in school. Then, after the kids get out of school at 3:47, we go pick up Fifi and bring her back home.

My mother-in-law has told us that at 3:30 every day, she takes Fifi outside to go to the bathroom and as soon as they come back in, Fifi runs to the door and waits for us. As soon as we open the door to get her, she jumps and wiggles with excitement. Once we get her back home, she energetically runs around the house, greeting each person and all three of our cats. And like clockwork, right about 5:00 she goes to the door to wait for my husband to get home from work so she can greet him, too.

While I was reflecting on Fifi's antics, Psalm 130:6 came to mind. Fifi waits for us more than the watchmen wait for the morning. But does my soul wait for the Lord the same way? Does yours? Psalm 130:5 says, "I wait for the Lord, my soul waits, and in His word I hope." But do our souls really wait for God?

While Fifi faithfully waits for us each day, I don't always look forward to my time in God's Word each day. Fifi never doubts that we will come for her, but sometimes when I petition God in prayer, I've already made up my mind that His answer is 'no.' I don't give God a chance to answer with a 'yes.' Instead of putting my hope in His Word, I put my faith in my own understanding.

Have you ever been there? Have you ever put your devotional time in like another chore on your to-do list? Have you ever half-heartedly gone to God in prayer?

If so, you are not alone. Thankfully, we have a God who loves us no matter what. Psalm 36:5 reminds us that God's steadfast love and faithfulness are with us always.

Even when we fail to put God first, He loves us to the cross and back. Even when our souls don't wait for Him, He never leaves us or forsakes us (Deuteronomy 31:6). Even when we doubt His goodness, He is good to us (Romans 8:28).

Today, Fifi has prompted me to pray for God to renew my love for Him so I look forward to my time with Him throughout the day. I'm praying for Him to fan into flame the Holy Spirit living in me (2 Timothy 1:6), so my soul waits for Him more than the watchmen wait for the morning. And more than Fifi waits for us. Will you join me in prayer?

My soul waits for the Lord more than watchmen for the morning,
more than watchmen for the morning.
Psalm 130:6 ESV

Prayer Moment:
Father God, Thank You for Your steadfast love and faithfulness to me. I come to You now to ask that You renew my heart for You. Don't let my love for You become lukewarm, Lord. Help me to fan into flame the gift of God in my soul, so my soul will wait for You more than the watchmen wait for the morning and more than Fifi waits for her people. In the name of Your Son, Jesus, I pray; Amen.

Heather Hart is a best-selling and award-winning author. God has given her a heart for ministering to women of all ages; helping them grow in their walk with Christ. Her goal isn't to tell others how to do more, be better, or achieve perfection, it's to point them to Jesus. Heather publishes daily devotions on her website DevotionForToday.com

17 Draw Close to Me

Danika Deva

Jazzy is snugging the door as closely as she can!

I recently got married and immediately became a dog mom and grandma at the same time. Woohoo! I'm hoping my new grandkids call me Gram-Cracker, but that hasn't happened yet! However, our big Aussie Shepherd barks to welcome me and wiggles her tail-missing hiney at me to show me love. In fact, she dog-talks to everyone who visits with a bark that is getting louder by the day. We think she is not able to hear her own bark even though she can hear the crinkle of a snack bag a mile away!

Our 12-year old dog, Jazzy, sticks closer to my husband than anyone. She follows him to the mailbox, the shed, the table and yes, even to the bathroom. She even follows him on the riding lawn mower as he cuts the grass, offering her frisbee to him around every turn.

One day I was watching her follow, follow, follow and had an "aha" moment. Has your dog ever brought those about for you? I wondered, "Shouldn't we stick so close to God like that?" We should be so close we will follow Him anywhere. Shouldn't we be glued to Him around every turn of life, even through the dark woods and deep waters of life?

In Scott's situation, Jazzy was there for him during cancer and the loss of his late wife. Jazzy helped carry him through a very tough time. Just like God, who does that for us. He carries us through our tough times, too.

> "Chase Jesus as hard as you chase the things that
> you think you want; you will wind up
> with more than you will ever need! "
> -Unknown

What stops us from getting as close to our Master as possible?
Not making God a priority?
The business of life?
Interruptions in life?
Wanting it my way and not His?
_____?

If you don't know, ask God to show you. He will and you can surrender it to Him.
It's never too late to lean into Jesus for everything! Just try it and see how He leans into you!

"Come close to God, and God will come close to you. Wash your hands, you sinners; purify your hearts, for your loyalty is divided between God and the world." James 4:8 NLT

Prayer Moment:
Lord, help me want to get as close to you as possible. Help me to love and read your Word, and to sit at your feet. Teach me to pray and wait expectantly. In Jesus' name, Amen.

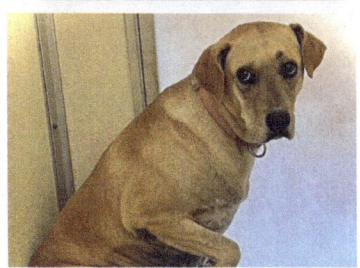

Other Books by Danika Deva

If you like this journal, check out more books at
www.DanikaDeva.com or on Amazon.com.

Newest Books
Operation Mission Plan (Military Devotional)
Journey to Who I Am in Christ
Journey to Hope Jail Journal
Figure It Out Journal: A Step-by-Step Process to Figure Anything Out

Power Journals for Kids!
My Living Things Journal
My Pet Rock
My Favorite Ponies, Horses, and Unicorn Sightings Journal
My Beautiful Butterfly Sightings Journal
My ABC Psalms for Kids Journal: Discovering God's Amazing Qualities
My Art Journal
My Beach Trip Journal

PowerJournals for Adults!
Pops of Joy Journal: Remembering the One you Love
Memories Matter Quilting Journal
Memories Matter My Memoir Creation Journal
Gone Fishin' Journal
Breakup Journal
Guitar Lover's Music Journal
Marvelous Music Journal
Figure It Out Journal: A Step-by-Step Process to Figure Anything Out

PowerJournals to Grow in your Walk with God!
The S.O.A.P. Journal: Scripture, Observation, Application and Prayer
My Memoir Journal: A Step-by-Step Guide to Write your Story
Freedom Sweep Journaling: Two-Way Conversations with the Father Through
Prayer
Journaling with the Father through Music: Connecting with the Father Through
Musical Reflection
My ABC Psalms Journal: Discovering the Attributes of God

Anthologies!
Kisses of Sunshine for Women
Cultivating Confidence from the Lord: in LIFE, through TRIALS, as
ENTREPRENEURS
Christmas with Jesus: 25 Devotions for December
The True Meaning of Joy: Devotional and Interactive Journaling

What a blessing it is "Taking 'Paws' to Reflect on God's Goodness" together!

If you enjoyed this book check out some of the other books, journeys and journals available on Amazon or at DanikaDeva.com.

Danika is a Jesus-loving, intentionally-living, principality-fighting, woman of God who delights in coaching others in the areas of business, hope, and life. As an educator and hope-dealer, she offers simple, life-changing solutions through her writing, speaking, and coaching.

Her God-given Ph.D. in "Hard Knocks" and "God Rocks" has equipped her to inspire others to "Be Intentional," and to choose joy and hope in hardship so they can not only heal, but flourish. She helps others "Get Unstuck from Yesterday's Yuck" with Freedom Sweeps, a five-step process to break through to freedom. You can learn more about Danika at DanikaDeva.com.

LET'S BE INTENTIONAL

BLESSINGS,

Made in the USA
Coppell, TX
06 December 2023